Love is Health

Published by: How To Love Ltd.

*"When the power of love overcomes the love of power,
the world will know peace."*
Jimi Hendrix

Table of Contents

Dualism

Since the beginning of time we have been told of the battle between the forces of good and evil. Super hero movies and Marvel comics depict these forces as external but what if this duel was actually taking place inside of you? Dualism exist to create a domain of orientation for finite expressions, your body is that expression. The nature of physical life is expressed in duality so that our choice will hopefully complete the indivisible trifecta - Father, Son, and Holy Spirit. Father, Son, and Holy Spirit is the same as mind, body, and spirit, not soul. Soul is the anchor to self that must be authenticated and merged with The Spirit. When Source created Earth, he created night to divide the day and so too our choices divide us from or bring us closer to the creator of all. Even in the day we find a middle ground, noon. You, we, soul, are the common ground at which our choices lie.

Polarity is the condition of physical life. We see that living organisms have two absolute options, that is to live or die therefore every decision brings us closer or further away from either or. You may say to yourself one cannot move away from physical death and it is true because death is inevitable. Yet one can prolong life which subsequently keeps you further away from death. You may say one cannot prolong life, but one can move to a city with less crime or eat a balanced diet and exercise, thus preserving the life. Therefore, we must consider how the eternal Spirit works in tandem to preserve the freedom of the soul. Preservation is the impact of choice.

In the world of information technology there is a binary number system which evaluates each number and translates it into a 1 or 0. So even in multi digit numbers they will only consist of 1's and 0's. You may think your choices have a range of outcomes, yet in reality they are just like this binary system, inching you closer to either a 1 or a 0, life or death, health or toxicity, heaven or hell, love or hate. The binary mode of thinking simplifies our rationale benefiting the human mind so we can stop overcomplicating the decision-making process.

When we activate binary thinking, we reverse engineer our problems and find the heart of the matter. Today, bombarded with choices, many choices are perceived as richness while lack thereof is seen as poverty. Yet the person experiencing more choices is prone to decision fatigue while less choices inadvertently edifies discipline and ease. Discipline creates freedom of mind. The more choices the less mental power. Eliminating unnecessary decisions lends more power for the mind to focus on matters of The Spirit.

Although our brain has 3 nodes of functioning, primal often referred to as lizard brain, limbic also known as mammal brain, and the neo cortex, our higher self, we often sway between the ego and higher self. The ego is a composition of the primal and mammal brain because these two lacks the discipline to delay gratification, catering to the justification of their desires and self-esteem. The primal brain focuses on survival, what we are going to eat, clothing, and shelter. While the mammal brain is concerned with pleasure and emotional validation. Devoid of higher order functioning the egocentric person exist happily in the 3-dimensional plane with little to no concern for ascending matters of The Spirit.

Contrarily, the neocortex is introspective relying on *innate* confidence and reason to choose wisely. Inner confidence has to be maintained in order to ascend. Nonetheless, by making primal and limbic choices predictable we can advance the ascension process to a new plane (4D, 5D, and so on) of consciousness via the neocortex. A lot of successful people have eliminated unnecessary choices from their lives by instilling rituals or principles to automate primal choices and limbic satisfaction. For example, eating the same breakfast every morning or waking up and going to bed at the same time is really grounding because it creates a reliable foundation for self. Reliability promotes confidence. Likewise, having a committed partner and/or social community automates the reception of emotional validation; which is beneficial in preventing the splintering of attention seeking behavior. Another instance is fashion, having such a strong impact on self-esteem may cause one to spend hours planning an outfit. Yet the energy of planning what to wear may be distracting to someone focused on ascension since a trademark for ascending is a deflated ego. Take Steve Jobs and Albert Einstein, who eradicated this issue by adhering to a simple uniform dress code. It's not to say a person focused on ascension doesn't care about their appearance it's just that its impact on self-worth is diminished due to the understanding of the physical world being only a manifestation of our inner world.

The motivation for our decisions is unconsciously based on the desire to meet a primal or emotional need. Because fulfilling primal or limbic needs briefly boosts our mood people overlook the root of the spiritual void they're overcompensating for. Thus, we need to invoke the Christ consciousness to evoke emotional intelligence. Emotional intelligence is the prerequisite for comprehension and ascension.

Satisfying the ego, for example, can cause impulsivity because the primal and limbic brain creates a detrimental state. Detrimental, means tending to cause harm, so the primal and limbic mind believes it is being harmed if this essential need is not met because the ego is being humbled. Here, sin is created, through an emotionally charged choice trying to meet a real need in an unhealthy way. Although I believe in the concept of sin as a means of explaining the nonlinear evolution of humanity I disagree with its religious context because it takes a derogatory tone. Learning to be disciplined is not a disposition to sin. It is the maturation of The Spirit. A child is born ignorant and that is natural not bad. The innate desires of the flesh and emotion have productive use but just like any new tool or skill must be trained. I liken the concept of sin to the miscalculation of needs and ignorance of healthy coping skills.

Romans 7:22 - "*My inner being delights in the law of God. But I see a different law at work in my body - a law that fights against the law which my mind approves of. It makes me a prisoner to the law of sin which is at work in my body.*" The misconception that we are prisoners of sin is an unevolved fallacy discounting the power of the mind and Spirit. Of course, if our passions are not moderated we risk casualties and addiction but the process of applying the habit of discipline is a simple act of evolution not an indication of an inherent error. This idea that we are born in iniquity (*Psalm 51*) completely refutes the purpose of life, which is to learn and claims that a child should be born mature, which is impossible.

Imagine a child, abandoned by a parent, the essential validation and love that comes from a parent wounds the inner child and if unmet causes them to crave satiation through promiscuous sex, obsession to achieve a high status or fame, over indulgence, and so forth. That is why the flesh is weak because it lacks the *ability* to truly rationalize and navigate emotion and desire.

Emotionally deprived people feel entitled to or desperate for physical intimacy, when in reality physical intimacy should be a derivative of spiritual intimacy. Intimacy of any kind can be established immediately. Like the rare occasion of meeting someone you feel like you've known forever. But why should it be a derivative? Because your physical vessel is sacred, it is the temple of all that is One - it is the final entry point to obtaining your full attention and relinquishing your full power. Once something or someone has gained access to your physical every facet of you can now be at its disposal unless you have systems in place to prevent that. When people are able to have one night stands it's because they have systems in place to detach their emotional functioning from physical connection. Knowing how to consciously do this is powerful but doing it unconsciously is dangerous because the optimal power of your vessel is obtained through full integration of all its facets: mental, physical, emotional, which collectively is spiritual. That is why when we consciously connect our breath (life force) to physical movement we feel intense engagement.

Practice: Somatic exercises

Understanding the science behind decision making reveals the polarity of life. One part of us, the ego, is focused solely on instant gratification or pleasure, the other on ascension. Either preserve life or death. Modulating brain functioning to a higher order reveals the illusion of choice. Free will is not real because choices are either instinctual or intuitive. The more the ego is developed, the more bodily instincts are heightened. Likewise, the more The Spirit ascends, the more intuition can override biological instincts. Romans 7:25 - *"This then is my condition: on my own I can serve God's law only with my mind, while my human nature serves the law of sin."* Who will you serve?

Emotions

Emotions make life worth living, they are the rollercoaster of life. Having access to every ride in the park is a prize. Source speaks to us through our emotions. When we ignore our feelings, we miss the opportunity to communicate with Source, to uncover and resolve an internal issue that God wants to heal. Dismissing emotions is ignoring Source contact. Emotional intelligence is the key to spiritual evolution and constitutes the evolved way of being. The more we develop emotional intelligence the more we secure ourselves in love. We become confident and our attachment style becomes secure (instead of ambivalent, avoidant, or disorganized) because we understand how to handle our inner most workings.

To develop emotional intelligence, you must be *in touch* with your inner child by exploring the subconscious mind because that is where you first experienced emotions. After all, the primary language of the subconscious mind *is* emotion. That is why the battle in life is yours alone because the war resides within. It seems unfair truly because the reason for our feelings or lack thereof is typically not the cause of anything we've done. Rather we are subject to circumstances, however unfortunate they are, meant to teach us how to love. Replace the victimization of subjection by developing the awareness to make your emotions an objectionable aspect of self. Conquer the enemy within and know true peace. The choice is yours. You can choose to oppress and suppress your emotions, which is God's direct access point to you. Or you can free yourself, win the war, by releasing trapped emotions through healthy self-expression.

Practice: Going through a rough patch? Become an objective party by talking to yourself out loud.

I recognize this is no easy feat because emotional abuse is something everyone has experienced whether indirectly or directly. Emotional abuse is a silent killer. It's hard to identify because we see abuse as active affliction but it is often withdrawal. Withdrawal of communication, withdrawal of participation, withdrawal of affection, etc. The abuse can be so impactful it causes emotional blindness which numbs our feelings or makes us scared of them. If we are not careful, we will unintentionally inflict the same abuse endured, on ourselves. The cycle of emotional abuse perpetuates through emotional neglect. The cause becomes the effect. Because you were emotionally abused you are more likely to emotionally neglect yourself or be emotionally abusive. Through awareness the cycle can be broken. Observe the one invisible force of all that is to understand the invisible power of feelings and achieve emotional freedom, the mental state of heaven.

The physical manifestation of feelings is expressed in and through the body (i.e. hormonal imbalance, metabolism, insulin resistance, and more.) therefore if not released self/soul will completely absorb itself resulting in narcissism, paranoia, and all other forms of radical internalization. Remember self-absorption is what created the most famous narcissist, the devil. So, we are righteously taught to die to self (ego) daily because if not we risk soul bondage and illness. *"...that, in reference to your former manner of life, you lay aside the old self, which is being corrupted in accordance with the lusts of deceit, and that you be renewed in the spirit of your mind, and put on the new self, which in the likeness of God has been created in righteousness and holiness of the truth."* - Ephesians 4:22-24

However, I don't believe in crucifixion. I believe in soul submission. The personality, the soul, must be merged with The Spirit via authentication. Crucifixion implies there is something about the primal human nature that needs to die but if God made us in his image and perfected us in our weakness (*Genesis 1:27 and 2 Corinthians 12:8-10*), our flesh is necessary. Primal instincts are what helped us evolve from hunter gatherers, but now as our basic needs are readily available we *must* train them to be satisfied in a healthy manner. Subsequently the emotional sphere becomes the outlier taking precedence in the acceleration of our evolution.

Pay attention to the sensations you feel in your body and this will lead you to an emotion. Follow the breadcrumbs. God will always leave a trail to find the hidden treasure.

For example, I normally feel anxiety in my stomach, pelvis, or groin, as a tight almost tingly sensation. I do not want that sensation to stay in my body so I have to move it up and out.

Practice: EFT tapping

Everything can be scaled, so the region of the stomach, pelvis, or groin are the lower chakras and thus *below* the heart and mind. Initiate the transcendental experience of ascending the scale from low to high by first becoming aware of it all (the situation, the context, the who, what, where, when, and why, if possible). Just as our feelings move us to tears, they too move us to action. Emotions are meant to put you in motion. It is no coincidence exercise improves mental health.

The consequence of sitting in emotions is illness because all that energy is being pressed in voluntarily (suppression), unconsciously (repression), or by force (oppression). On the other hand, balance, sometimes you do need to sit in your feelings to effectively process. Think about a computer buffering. Eventually the data will get to its right destination or else the process will have to be restarted. In severe cases a computer may freeze and have to be shut off if it buffers too long. And so, a human unable to process emotions (communication from Source), will completely detach from God and healthy emotional functioning, stunting the evolution of love (health).

Regardless you must express to expel and manifest. If you are not emotionally intelligent you will incorrectly process life. Everything will be misinterpreted and cultivate the range of low vibrational energies such as guilt, shame, insecurity, etc. Alternatively, you may misinterpret evil for good unable to discern signs of danger. The ability to connect the dots will be disrupted corrupting confidence in source, self, and authentication of soul. Harriet Tubman said "I freed a thousand slaves. I could have freed a thousand more if they knew they were slaves." Without emotional intelligence and control you are a slave to the ego. It may not look or feel like it because superficial needs are met but in reality, your soul is in bondage to the inflation of self-esteem and/or comfort. Imagine a computer with a virus, on the outside it looks perfectly healthy but is in fact infected. Moreover, every action taken with said device is a liability. A computer has processors to interpret data correctly, humans have emotions.

Forbearance

Relations are built in connections that must be fortified through time. Surely connections can be instant but their operation is *tentative*. Operation requires forbearance, tried and true effort from all parties involved. How much effort are you putting into your relationship with God? How badly do you want to connect with source? Because Earth is not the original home of The Spirit that dwells within, the soul, longs to be fully authenticated in order to remember the source of which it came from. Through various practices we play the process of elimination until the connection to God is fortified.

The ultimate experience of God comes from the intentional experiment of love (health). Keep experimenting that is the effort which will reveal God to you, you to you. The character of a person is built on what they perpetually pursue. Putting in effort without regard for the outcome builds integrity. If acts of kindness are only done to receive praise or reward is the character of that person truly kind or manipulative? Which is why we must tread lightly with religious or spiritual devotions ensuring that our practices are in tune with the most high and not the result of an inferiority complex. Consistent internal checks will become routine maintenance but can be exhausting because once we ascribe to a practice or religion this idealized version of ourselves is imagined. Fantasizing about the realization of our idealized self creates a deep yearning that grows with emotional attachment. Becoming emotionally attached to the imagination creates a void in reality causing the operation of lack. One must emotionally detach from the aim and simply persist because the effort alone grants confidence from endurance although endurance does not bring increase. Your increase has a specific due date God has predestined and *how* you wait to receive it indicates whether or not you are ready.

Forbearance is a virtue we must learn because we need to know how to stand for a promise. We need to know how to stand firm in the faith! *Faith moves mountains and forbearance stirs faith.* This is not a job we can take lying down. Standing is the protest the opposition hates to see. Protests affirms belief in the promise. When people are protesting in the streets they are disrupting traffic and business as usual, they are marching down streets with signs demanding justice. Learn to disrupt and ignore doubt through long suffering because faith will dwindle and when it does you must persist toward the promise to bring yourself in alignment. Long suffering doesn't have to mean that you're sitting in pain but it does mean you've sat in a state unchanged. When a situation is not changing *you* have to change. The ruling force of your being has to change to love.

The key to forbearance is pace. A seed doesn't sprout overnight. Observing nature shows us how plants grow without question, irrespective of the universal elements used in its development. A plant knows to photosynthesize sunlight but is not responsible for the sun. And so, the pace of bloom is contingent upon the weather. Therefore, do not glorify the works of your hands expecting the law of cause and effect to instantly apply if you have not delivered and submitted all expectation of outcome to God. We do not serve an emotionless God. We serve a God with a loving personality; so, we can say in full assurance of our friendship with God that we have the ability to move him.

The creator of all is waiting for the perfect opportunity to meet us where our efforts max out. Galatians 6:9 says *"Let us not grow weary of doing good, for at the proper time we will reap a harvest if we do not give up."* Exhausted of all options we are left in a state of surrender yet equipped with the aligning habits to our desired reality; whereby emotional freedom is sustained because the inner confidence from said aligned behavior and God's credible nature reassures us of its fruition.

Hate is Toxic

To live regard both love and hate as necessary after all suffering comes from both. To die spiritually, however, is the disregard for emotional intimacy, intelligence, and freedom, which is love. *Love doesn't always feel good and hate doesn't always hurt.* Hate is the toxic force that binds the soul. It stunts healthy spiritual matriculation. Hate is a prison clinging to selfish ambition producing fear. Hate shrinks soul, perception, and emotional aptitude until finally the person is completely blind and void. Blind, as in unable to perceive and interpret true contact from God and life in a healthy manner; and void, empty of loving creative expression.

The two primary nodes of hate are greed and isolation. Isolation happens when the negative state of insecurity has been reached. Insecurity causes misinterpretation and its pinnacle, delusion. Greed, the positive state of insecurity, requires constant feeding to affirm its view, this is why misery loves company. Although we are naturally social creatures love can thrive, that is emotionally regulate and evolve regardless of companionship.

Living in a perverse world confuses the being. Hate is tolerated because people are confused. We call bad good and good bad. Appeals to our primal urges however valid they maybe are glamorized - from colorful candy wrappers to enticing rock stars; if sin didn't feel good everyone would be free. While love mandates tedious tasks and ample effort, delaying gratification, hate releases inhibitions at first only to imprison you later, hence addiction. The insatiable self-absorbed soul looking for love in all the wrong places. Psalms 42:1 - *"I long to drink of you O'God, to drink deeply from the streams of pleasure flowing from your presence. My longing overwhelms me for more of you."* Hate destroys healthy consumption and perception. Hate is intelligent but expiring. Hate cannot transcend and adapt to the change of time positively, sentencing the soul to bondage. In order for a soul to be free it must authenticate and merge with The Spirit. Because the soul is the blueprint for personality it can be fickle and deceptive misguiding you away from The Spirit. Soul searching is the journey to learn the authentic nature of self. While soul selling is the defamation of persona. *"It is worthless to have the whole world if they lose their souls…"* - Matthew 16:26. An inauthentic persona does not have the aptitude to limitlessly transact love.

Fear, usually irrational, but hate ruminates on its subject and devises a plot. Because of hates intelligence and ability to hyper focus it can be dangerously powerful. We've seen its power in the form of slavery and genocide and want nothing more to abolish the people or policies that allowed this to happen. I'd argue that'd do us a disservice because whenever there is an opportunity to hate there is a bigger opportunity to love. Hate is a necessary evil for awakening to The Truth. It is the night to divide the day. If we didn't have a polar opposite of love we would never know what it is. If slavery didn't exist would we value freedom the same? Hate has a place and those who *are* love use it to their benefit.

How can we benefit from hate? Our reflexes *can* be trained to love the more toxicity we experience. Because it is natural to combat hate with hate, we must defy nature; you've been told to fight fire with fire but it is water that extinguishes the flames. Anytime we grow in love we must defy a natural instinct in a healthy way. When you are met with a negative comment you become offended. The natural reflex is to defend yourself. Rebuke the inclination and realize your weapons are depersonalization, reflection, and deflection. When hate manifest you have to defy the natural reaction to absorb its energy. Be a mirror so that you reflect the opposite or else you risk internalization. Self-implosion is the result of internalization, decaying emotional processing, and killing aptitude. Eventually the only emotions left to recall are all low vibrational and default operation will be reduced to a constant state of desire and lack because valid needs are being exploited by fear. How people treat you is a representation of how much emotional intelligence they've developed. Free people, emotionally secure people, function with the knowledge of oneness. Know that we all come from one source and therefore we recognize and respect the divinity in all.

Love is health

According to Kendra Cherry "Love is a set of emotions and behaviors characterized by intimacy, passion, and commitment. It involves care, closeness, protectiveness, attraction, affection, and trust." Abusive relationships contain all these attributes so what's the difference? I mean if love were so easily defined surely, we'd have the hang of it by now. Fed *fairytales* and romcoms from birth honest efforts have been made to sell us the figments of someone else's imagination, *not* love. Anyone can define love for you when you choose to stop seeking the experience yourself.

Love is the state of emotional security and freedom. Love is the *absolute* force that transmutes all to total health. Love is freeing. Love is divine acceptance. When I say I love you that means I heal you. If "love" is not healing then it is not. This topic is often approached as some woo woo new age science project yet it's anything but.

Love has to be viewed from the dualist angle of healthy verse toxic because we need extremist scales to balance average events into perspective. Western philosophers such as Plato and Aristotle deemed this the 'Golden Mean'. In this regard a middle ground is what balances the disproportion of two extremes. Your soul (personality) is the middle ground. So, the evidence of eating salad instead of a box of donuts is without a doubt an act of love but one donut won't hurt (depending on your condition).

In scripture Paul defines love with visible qualities *"Love is patient, love is kind. It does not envy, it does not boast, it is not proud. It does not dishonor others, it is not self-seeking, it is not easily angered, it keeps no record of wrongs. Love does not delight in evil but rejoices with the truth. It always protects, always trusts, always hopes, always perseveres."* - 1 Corinthians 13:4-8

The fruits of the Holy Spirit embody the highest vibrations such as: patience, kindness, gentleness, forbearance, joy, peace, self-control, and faithfulness. Other "sources" of "love" become obsolete because The One, Holy Spirit contains every facet of love imaginable. Yet these expressions of love are not love itself because of the reality of dualism. Something so pure can be weaponized turning a simple act of kindness into a form of manipulation. We are all at risk of being love bombed and the three main suspects are affection, attention, and attraction. While all three are natural manifestations of love, alone, it is not.

Byproducts of love are not absolute and its efficacy is contingent upon the void emotional intelligence, and attachment style of the person. The voids we house are pitfalls in self and soul that cause us to outsource love. We all have voids, holes in our design because somewhere along the way our self-esteem was shot. This is not to say affection, attention, and attraction, are useless but to a more secure person they carry less weight. An emotionally intelligent person is able to look objectively during these instances and not be "swept off their feet". How do these three integral components become the exploitation of love?

Attraction pleases biology but *behooves* the spirit. Most people think attraction equates to sexuality claiming that sexuality is a spectrum. In reality attraction is the spectrum while sexuality is definitive because you can appreciate a product without committing to a purchase. Attraction is the superficial headliner of relationships and can be manifested by something as simple as proximity. Exposure effect is the influence of proximity. Therefore the more we are exposed to a person, a lifestyle, an activity the higher the probability of liking it. So how do you know if attraction is genuine?

Practice: Observe the context and ask yourself if such and such was not a factor would I still want or like this? Example: If I really believed in myself would I still be working this job?

If you see a commercial enough times eventually you cave into trying the product. So how do you know if attraction is genuine? Genuine attraction will speak to The Spirit and *encourage* inner confidence and peace because The Spirit speaks to all (mental, emotional, and physical).

Secondly, affection, which we are fed so much of as babies suddenly fades away per adulthood. Do we stop needing that much affection as we grow older? I don't believe so. In fact, I believe we may need it even more. I've heard the best adult maintains their inner child and innocent affection aside curious creation will achieve just that. Unfortunately, desperate lengths to achieve this balance make the rising norm of touch deprivation an obstacle and proponent to promiscuity. Touch deprivation can lead to serious health issues that's why I'm not shaming anyone's game because affection, smothering kisses and big bear hugs are scientifically proven to be good for you. Science has proved highly affectionate relationships have health benefits ranging from lower stress to lower cholesterol. Nonetheless we should be mindful of the scale love (health), hate (toxic), objectively probing ourselves to ensure the yearn for affection isn't some hollow attempt to cope.

Maybe the biggest threat of them all, attention. "Energy goes where attention flows" - Tony Robbins. What is the correlation between attention and entertainment? Attention is the price we pay to be entertained. If you break the word entertainment down we see an entrance to obtain. Contrary to every reality television shows quest for love, this invaluable force is not here for mere entertainment but perfecting healthy growth. Attention is the leverage used for control, *it's the price paid for power.* When something has power over you it has your attention. In relationships, power dynamics are quickly established through communication. Texting, for instance, often induces anxiety because we live in an overly accessible time. There are too many ways to get a hold of someone and we've become entitled to communication or attention. Waiting for one person to respond can feel like an eternity nowadays, especially when people are strategically planning out their response ensuring they don't respond to soon or too late, when they finally do a dopamine response is now connected to their point of contact and easily misinterpreted as love. Endorphins should be released when you're connecting with someone you like just be aware it's not being exploited or manipulated. I'm not sure who said it but there's a concept that children spell love with time. So, the more time spent on a matter the more it is cultivated. Make sure you are cultivating health.

Do you spend enough time living in the awareness of all that is? Because if not true love will feel foreign. The Holy Spirit enters you so that two become one and then Source love becomes self-love. True love only feels long distance because you create the distance. You distance yourself from your emotions by burying them under entertainment, comfort food, or work. The distance persists the more we try to escape from ourselves. God wants to spend time with you but he can't when you fill your schedule to the brim. When you leave no room to bring awareness to or evaluate your feelings and behavior, you leave no room for God. Leave room for God by sitting in silence, journaling, learning, meditating (meditation is any healthy practice which delivers your mind into bliss and stillness i.e. exercising or breath work), and worshipping, which is any act of reverence and adoration to source (ex. singing or dancing) so his love can unfold solidifying the wisdom in you to know the difference.

With this new-found awareness we can now remove the *subject* of love, you, and look objectively. A Cleveland Clinic article states "Love bombing is a form of psychological and emotional abuse that involves a person going above and beyond for you in an effort to manipulate you into a relationship with them." These conduits manipulate your mind into believing someone really cares for you. Each conduit has a dual outcome. Affection and attraction can turn into lust. Attention can turn into distraction. Gifts can turn into entitlement or greed. Victims of love bombing may fall head over heels because they are either unaware or playing out some fantasy in their head. But not you, no, you practice discernment. You think objectively. You develop and trust your intuition. Because there's century's worth of deprogramming we have to do in order to even the scales. In order to reprogram the concept of love you first need to analyze your media consumption and just consumption in general. Are the songs and shows you watch perpetuating toxicity or health?

Speaking of, let's dissect Twilight, a movie which has become a beloved classic for many everywhere, and one of the most toxic displays of love, ever. As much as I love Twilight I can't get down with the mindset being perpetuated. If you haven't seen it the story entangles Bella, a reserved high school student who moves to a new state to live with her dad, and Edward the local vampire dream boat. As the plot would have it the two fall for each other after Edward saves her not once but twice from life threatening danger. The damsel in distress archetype is reinforced and through various phases of hard to get they become inseparable. That is until Edward decides to break up with Bella because "she doesn't belong in his world". After all he is a vampire and although he doesn't eat humans anymore he is very tempted by Bella's blood. Bella becomes an adrenaline junkie with severe depression because whenever she's doing something reckless is when she sees glimpses of Edward in her mind. Can we love ourselves enough to value our wellbeing before that of a relationship? She literally gives up her soul to be with this man. Consider your soul because it is definitely necessary to evolve in love.

Defiance of The Spirit is the act of selfish ambition. Bella put her life in danger to win back her boyfriend. Stuck in the primal mind she was unable to transmute her feelings up the scale, to the higher chakras (heart and mind) to rationalize the situation causing her to believe the illusion of detriment. Acting on our primal impulses is often a cry for help. Someone in their *right* mind will pursue health. Unless you're trying to save someone's life from physical danger, valuing something or someone over your wellbeing and God is pure idolatry. There is a time and place for heroics but only a sound person can correctly asses that because although you can save a physical body you can't heal a soul. Healing is a personal choice to lovingly apply all the tools you've been given. Bella's health, the fate of her life, was crippled in the hands of Edward because she lacked self-worth and self-love. Every living entity falls short of the glory of God (*Romans 3:23*) but never should you feel shocked to be receiving love because that is your *birthright*. You are inherently loveable. You are inherently worthy of love despite your shortcomings.

Yet this is why idolizing has been embedded in us because we were born into ignorance and trained to hate ourselves. Hyper aware of our flaws, we shamefully clothe ourselves with leaves, hiding from true connection to Source. Naturally when self-esteem and worth are not built on the solid foundation (Christ consciousness) we are vulnerable to bow to idolatry. Apart from God, left with idols, there the *outsource* of love. Knowledge of error should not revoke confidence but it does. We know Bella had low confidence because she referred to herself as "Nothing. Human." Humans are powerful multidimensional beings, we are designed to be the physical manifestation of God, and thus we could never be nothing. She also couldn't fathom being loved by Edward. Similar to effects of celebrity culture she made Edward her God. Idolatry blindly outsources love, foolishly ignoring red flags and placing needs and desires in the hands of something less than God; while true love is a transparent commitment to source.

Although the community Bella had was outraged at her behavior, her sense of self was blindsided by this affair trapped in astute tunnel vision. Tunnel vision is necessary when dedicating your life to purpose. But purpose is never solely a person, rather what you are to learn from a person. In Bella's time of distress, she internalized her feelings fearfully clinging to the past instead of accepting it and letting go. Too much focus on any space and time but the present is a distraction inducing fear. Love knows when and how to set boundaries to keep you present because the present is the only moment we are completely free to create. Let your wellbeing and healthy evolution be the perpetual present focus so that it becomes an unapproachable boundary because love starts with you. God, love, would never jeopardize your livelihood. Because love is not self-seeking. Love is health seeking.

The Alpha and Omega is the only one acceptable to have selfish love. Source wants us all to his self because in being with him we adopt his way of perfection to become the physical manifestation of God. He has the right to be that way because he created us. Yielding to his selfishness we become selfless. When you give God's right authority of selfishness away to someone or something else you lose the authentic awareness of connection to source and begin outsourcing love via idolatry. Establishing the emotional security of love is the only way to prevent this behavior. Any love you experience from friends, family and romantic partners is an extension of the love God has given you and establishing within you. An ordained partnership will seek God's will first and foremost whether it requires them being separate or together. A worldly partnership seeks personal will together or individually. In short, love is not some obscure or imaginary thing. It is concrete and evident. It is alive and well but can be skewed with: media, community, and lastly self. Media reinforces community and both reinforce self. Subsequently we inevitably face two crises: existential and identical.

Crises

Existential crises are the skew of purpose while identity crises are the skew of self. Skewed perceptions feed questions. Seek affirming experiences and the questions cease. We have to experience life affirmatively, that is with confidence. If there is nothing you are confident about then you are still in training. Confidence doesn't only come from achievements of big success but of daily ordinary tasks, like brushing your teeth. Self-care is a privilege that fortifies our individuality and confidence. Yet even confidence is not enough to ensure love is unfolding because the double-edged sword of the inflated ego can mislead you.

We come into this world training to be of service to Source but The Spirit within must be confident enough to do so. Trauma causes us to question what that service is. Keep finding things that fill you with love, that authenticate your soul, so that one day it may become your service. If you are unsure what fills you with love, you too are still in training and need to experience more. The more life you experience the more your purpose and identity unfolds. Purpose and identity are inherent. Its unique expression is found at the feet of God surrendered of expectations and desires. Delivered from human wisdom we understand, just because a skill is mastered does not make that your purpose. And just because we have a job title does not make that our identity.

Existential Crises

You have been personally called to specific assignments by The Creator. Nonetheless, it is easy to get confused on what the assignments are because we are over stimulated with media, often comparing our lives to celebrities or others we admire. In other cases, people assign us their perception and we feel an obligation to live up to traditional expectations. The option to reject invalid assignments is always available but not accessible because the art of peer pressure weakens the knees and bends to please. Invite the authority to reject by learning to go within. Be pro self. You can't be pro self if you don't even know who you are or what you want. Who you are is beguiled by what you consume and verified by what you create. Once you solve the riddle of you, there will come a point in time where you have to deny self(ego) for the sake of God's will. Being alone in his presence (silence/nature) will clear your vessel. Comparison will cease when contentment begins.

Solitude is the first step to solving the existential crises. You must first be content with yourself before finding it in others. In solitude we discover we are never really alone. We are either unaware *or* aware of his presence. Being in a perpetual state of awareness of his presence and modeling yourself after bearing witness to his character is how to partner with God. Upon reaching said awareness, the invisible influence on the visible establishes a *reverent* interaction. Reverence of God quiets the crises and segways to purpose. *Because God is almighty and therefore all purposeful you too obtain purpose by association.* Partnership with The Creator brings eternal fulfillment and each fruit of love unlocks every level to the ascending identity and purpose.

Contrarily living without purpose can be necessary to understand both sides of the coin. It's kind of like that saying "you don't know what you got til its gone" So while it's gone what you don't have becomes more and more apparent and therefore your thirst for it grows. Living without purpose awakens the need for a drive because you are going places, you just need a compass, a guide to get you there, and that guide is love. The uselessness felt will be nullified as every interaction becomes a calibration of the compass calling us back to our original purpose which is to be his loving child. Your first reason for existing is to be his loving child. Are you living as a child of God? Babies do not wonder too far ahead into the future, they are not concerned for their next meal, because these things are a given. This is the choice you have to make. Choose to be His child or go your own way.

A self-righteous personality will inevitably experience fear-based programs causing the branch to separate from the vine. *"I am the vine; you are the branches. If you remain in me and I in you, you will bear much fruit; apart from me you can do nothing."* - John 15:5 what prevents us from becoming a child again are expectations. We believe we should be further in life because we got that degree. We believe we should be married by now because most people our age are. Our beliefs are results of comparisons and ingrained *world* standards that need to be dismantled.

How do you dismantle a belief system? By realizing the error, isolating it, and combatting it with the truth, which is found in health. It is an ongoing process requiring diligence. Love does its due diligence. What if the only thing you were called to do was love? Would you be up for the task? That is how you should exist, as if your only purpose is to love. Existing in this way refutes all expressions of fear. Existing in this way sets the tone of confidence and responsibility required to steward purpose.

Identity Crisis

It's hard to believe you are a child of God when "born into sin". Never does life come short of mistakes but when we make those mistakes it's a blow to our confidence. I look back on choices I've made and I feel so guilty, so ashamed and I question God, how can I be yours? We perceive children as pure and blameless due to their innocence, so how can that be you when you've sinned on purpose? We receive the benefit of the doubt because the grace of God covers a multitude of sins we are able to find ourselves at the receipt of his forgiveness and mercy. For *"Great is his faithfulness; his mercies begin afresh each morning."* - Lamentations 3:23

The enemy will tell us differently and conjure up an illusion. "The enemy knows your name, but calls you by your sin. God knows your sin but calls you by your name."- Ricardo Sanchez. In good faith we must believe *"... that nothing can ever separate us from God's love. Neither death nor life, neither angels nor demons, neither our fears for today nor our worries about tomorrow—not even the powers of hell can separate us from God's love."- Romans 8:38* in all our flaws God honors the part of us that continues to hold ourselves accountable for our actions and pursue health.

We struggle to believe our identity when we don't know who our maker is. *When you forget who you are remember who God is.* And how do we understand who The Creator is? By observing their character, by bearing witness to love.

Practice: Go outside. Observe and research nature because that is pure evidence of The Divine's intelligent character at work.

You may never have all the pieces to the puzzle that is you but you will have enough to see the grand scheme.

The grand scheme, the big picture, is health. Diasporas lay in our consciousness leaving us fixated on physical identity. However, your spiritual identity trumps any physical identification assigned to you. The world may classify you with race or economic status but it is The Spirit within that animates your life.

Did you know adopted children are more likely to struggle with identity due to information gaps in their history? And so, as we are reinitiated into the kingdom of God we acknowledge these missing links and wonder how did I get here? Why me? Is this right for me? We start to question our place and value even though we come from a place of value. You are inherently valuable. Where you are right now is the place where God needs to meet you. I believe we expect God or purpose or identity to be revealed only after we have met some man-made criteria. We say I will meet God after I've completed this fast, or after I stop drinking. So, the human condition of the world imposes achievement to receive but God is in the midst regardless. God needs acknowledgement not achievement. Acknowledge me as The Source, acknowledge me as your maker he says and you will know who I am and thus you will find out who you are.

The surface level of identity is the product of everything you think, say, and do. "The soul becomes dyed with the color of its thoughts" - Marcus Aurelius. Although not every thought is a definitive declaration to who you are at your core. In fact, we have over 35,000 thoughts a day so the totality of our thoughts can be dismissed because it's most likely subconscious garbage. That's why it's so important to be a vigilant consumer and critical thinker. It is up to you to take every thought captive and make it obedient to Christ (*2 Corinthians 10:5*). Identity must be perceived through action or being and healthy action will only come from a healthy mind and way.

Practice: For every negative thought combat it with three positives as it relates to the subject.

If God spoke and it was so then words shape reality. Much research has proven the power of positive self-talk. The 'top down approach' refers to the ability of language to travel from the prefrontal cortex to the subconscious with declarative statements which reshape perception. *"Thus the mouth speaks what the heart is full of. Speech of a good man brings good things out of the good stored up in his heart, and an evil man brings evil things out of the evil stored up in his heart"*- Luke 6:45. Speak life over all.

Distraction

The opposition we face on the journey is distraction because it obscures identity. Scripture says we do not wrestle against flesh and blood but of the principalities and rulers of the world which exploit our vulnerabilities. The cosmetic and entertainment industry for example bank on our insecurities. Not rich enough? Tune in to a reality show so you can vicariously live through someone else. Feeling ugly? How about you spend money you don't have to wear designer brands.

Practice: Imagine all the money you invested into escaping reality or inflating ego was actually used to deploy healthy strategies to change it.

While there are dark forces here on Earth that should be none of our *concern* because the protection of the most high never leaves us. Sometimes religion does us a disservice in bringing too much attention to darkness. The education is necessary the constant reminder is the distraction invoking fear. The sooner we take responsibility for the micro (self) we can change the macro (world).

Unless we obtain emotional security via the Holy Spirit we will continue to be distracted. The Spirit affirms. The flesh wonders. My soul wants to spend time with God but my flesh thinks he is boring. The age of instant gratification has warped our dopamine functioning, the reward, the pleasure receipt is what we seek.

Relationships are not sought. The benefits of relationships are sought after. Seeking pleasure is the desire of the flesh which distracts from fortifying connection, the pursuit of The Spirit.

Moreover, because the benefits of your relationship with God do not come as quickly as the dopamine hit of worldly pleasures you do not withstand. Steadfast love withstands a true relationship. This is why even in all our mistakes God says he will never leave us or forsake us (*Hebrews 13:5*). At times distractions cause us to forsake God unknowingly but with vigilance we can persevere receiving the reward of Source (love). Is the blessing you want a distraction from the relationship you need? Can your relationship survive without the reward? The test of time reveals where your heart lies. When the blessing distracts from the connection the relation is false.

Distractions evade vulnerability. A true relationship allows vulnerability to nurture. Vulnerability is the prelude to enlightenment. Truly knowing thyself is experiencing the intimacy of vulnerability. One must be in touch with self before they can consciously touch another soul. Although his ways are not our ways, in the practice of divine acceptance we adopt his ways, establishing the viable intimacy to sustain his character. This unfolding allows us to surpass the distraction of confrontation and find peace in the processing of the relationship.

Sitting in the process is the dark night of the soul, the void of silence. The process is the interim between illumination and complete union. It feels uncomfortably stagnant. It feels like a personal attack. Something about sitting in the midst of his silence amplifies everyone else's blessings. There's nothing to do with silence but sit. Silence will be unbearable when you don't know to do that. Just sit in the silence provided. Just *be* quiet. Silence your desires, silence the flesh, and *sit* in the silence. Silence speaks. Can you handle the silence or will you distract yourself with life's nuances? We desire to be distracted because we can't handle the way we feel or the uncertainty of the unknown. We don't want to unpack it so we distract ourselves with *entertainment*. Silence is an invitation to stillness because in silence is the pure confidence of love.

Think about it in new relationships, when we're getting to know someone we want to keep the conversation going on and dread the inevitable space of silence because it's uncomfortable to sit in silence with someone we don't know. We talk aimlessly to avoid it yet with someone we have history with we can nestle in the silence and situate ourselves just fine. Sitting in silence is a testimony to the firm relationship you have built and the magnitude of its bond. Silence relieves distraction.

The silence speaks and Abba says "What is so wrong about just being with me?" My flesh replies "Because you're not fun God. You're not sexy or cool and you bring up things I don't want to feel. I don't want to feel bored or *alone* but I am all the time because I don't *feel* you and I'm mad that you don't fill me up like food does." Replace your plate with prana (breath). It's not always going to *feel* like God is there but when we take a breath we're reminded of his omnipotence. Breathe through the distractions.

Discipline

The only discipline you need is to keep going. Keep going even though you don't see the result you want. Push pass the frustration of the flesh. The flesh will try to move on to something that instantly gratifies. *But let the craving of The Spirit outweigh the desire of the flesh.* Let the longing for Source outweigh the curiosity to roam. Because we are not wanderers we are explorers. *A wanderer roams with the whims of desire. An explorer strategically searches.* The explorer receives the experience of God through the experiment of love. The root of resolution to our identity crises lies at the realization of two definitions: Discipline that is dedication. Love, which is health. The moment you dedicate your life to health, you become a co-creator with all that is instead of a mere bystander.

Value must be ascertained to dedicate. In all the virtues acquired awareness is at the forefront of its development and discipline at the core of its maintenance. I fast a lot to discipline my flesh. Initially, I thought failing to complete a fast or sustain my eating plan was lack of discipline but it was often lack of coordination between healthy coping skills and challenges. The reality is that the practice alone submits the flesh to The Spirit and each point of failure is only preparation to do better next time. If you haven't reached your destination then do not stop training. Keep going that is the discipline.

There are going to be times when we fail when we give up but that is literally *beside* the point. Every situation that simulates failure is an opportunity for the fruits of The One to abound in you. Failure does not constitute quitting. Failure constitutes preparation. In order to fail you must not be ready to win yet. I've failed many times to complete a fast and I have completed many fast but in times of failure I never once decide to not do it anymore. Someone said "Success is where preparation meets opportunity", so continue to prepare until you can seize the opportunity.

We are never short of an opportunity to discipline ourselves. Recognize that every aspect of life can be disciplined. Eating, waking up to bed time, work, it all can be disciplined. The question is what's the point? The point is to be measured. A cake is not baked without the precise measurements to perfect its texture and taste. Likewise, we must *measure* our lives by the ruler of love because lack of moderation stretches our morals thin.

Minimalism is a good system of discipline to have because similar to fasting it starves pleasure. Today living in a capitalistic society there is an unhinged longing for the next best thing. Self-denial to worldly pleasures reinforces the truth of existence, which is that we cannot take any of this with us when our physical bodies die. The only thing that carries over spiritually are the lessons we have or have not learned. Minimalism begs to question "Is this necessary?" most of the time the answer is no.

Another good system to have in place is a creation to consumption ratio. I use the 2:1 ratio, creating double the amount I consume. The mind and The Spirit must always be developed more than the physical. Until we train our minds to be focused on The Spirit we will not increase physically. In the place of physical restraint (limitation), the mind, The Spirit has the option to expand. When there is too much access to the physical, The Spirit, the mind, will diminish because consumption becomes a distraction.

Lifestyle

'The way The truth The life' is a mantra taught by Yeshuah which people often misinterpret by believing there is only one way to heaven or to connect with Source. And in some respect that is true because *fortification* to Source comes from the experiment of love but that experiment looks different for everyone. What is healthy for you may not be beneficial to another. This scripture is simply highlighting the importance of focusing on how you live your life and to do it in a truthfully healthy manner. Love is the lifestyle of healing, it is not just a feeling it's a practice. Practicing health in *all* relations calibrates you to love.

The way you live is a mirror to the systems and/or spirits operating within you. Although these systems may have been installed within due to trauma or genetics their operation is in accordance to the obedience of either the flesh(ego) or The Spirit. Because Spirit is the animating force of life if The One Holy Spirit is not functioning within (because there are many spirits) the vessel reverts back to default setting, human nature. Human nature is of the flesh, we know it has its place but alone cannot transcend to pure love. Therefore, what resonates with your soul and spirit doesn't always agree to influence because it may not be able to override the default. For example, growing up in an abusive household may foster programs of insecurity and anger and thus the aim of your lifestyle is to cope with the damage; however, lacking the education, the coping skills chosen are unhealthy and therefore obey the flesh. Lifestyle supersedes resonation because innate programs are operating within that *distract* the purity of Christ consciousness.

As an adolescent I never received consistent emotional validation. This led me to unhealthy coping mechanisms such as self-harm and over indulgent behavior. Leading well into my 20's I was a sufficient party goer, enjoying recreational drugs regularly- by chance, by miracle, I had a spiritual encounter during one of these episodes and the urge to smoke completely left me. However, it was a profound lack of emotional intelligence that got me there. Ignorance promotes harm. Comprehending the motive of your choices enlightens the reason. This is the process of living in love - observing to understand.

Practice: Ask yourself why you do what you do.

Are you correctly interpreting your observations? Congenital insensitivity to pain is a disorder that inhibits individuals from feeling pain, comparable to the protective measure the brain has for blocking traumatic memories, the ability to recognize danger or toxicity may be inactive due to these conditions that have created an imbalance in receptors, desensitizing your reception of pain and exploiting those of pleasure. Normally when our body is in pain that signals to the mind and The Spirit that something requires healing. In an imbalanced person this will be misinterpreted instead signaling to the mind a need for pleasure. Life isn't meant to be perpetually painful, the pain should help steer us toward health. People will have trouble steering because a.) They haven't learned what health is b.) They are not processing pain efficiently c.) Or the soul needs to merge with The Spirit so that God can steer. It can be necessary for us to walk a lifestyle of destruction to send out an SOS. It's funny we think we don't need love. We think money or sex or friends will satisfy us but even the richest people commit suicide. Love won't strike us as vital until we become aware of what it is. Love is health. All life is *sustained* by it.

The more I experienced the opposite of love the more I became aware I was missing something. Like a head held underwater I started gasping for air. Everyone knows the value of air and every moment spent not healing is living with a held breath. Thus, we need to induce a conscious breath to keep the love within fluid. Love is the state of flow and conscious breathing gets you there. Conscious breathing is the act of surrendering to the present space and time. Pranic healing is a holistic practice which uses the breath to restore balance in the body. Prana refers to the vital life force flowing through all (some often refer to that vital life force as spirit.) It seems too good to be true yet there are breathing techniques to help us through every situation, even painful ones like pregnancy. Learning to breathe correctly and with the pure intention to heal will keep the energy within on a continuum. Love

is the continuum of life recycled through breath it flows
freely.

Notes

1.   Cherry, Kendra. "Is Love Biological or Is It a Cultural Phenomenon?" Very Well Mind, 2020, www.verywellmind.com/what-is-love-2795343.
2.   Cleveland clinic. "What Is Love Bombing? 7 Signs to Look For." Cleveland Clinic, 31 Jan. 2023, health.clevelandclinic.org/love-bombing.

www.ingramcontent.com/pod-product-compliance
Lightning Source LLC
Chambersburg PA
CBHW060913130726
48001CB00006B/2215